BOA
EDITIONS
LIMITED

THE ORCHARD

THE ORCHARD

Poems by
Brigit Pegeen Kelly

AMERICAN POETS CONTINUUM SERIES, NO. 82

BOA Editions Ltd. ~ Rochester, NY ~ 2004

First Edition
04 05 06 07 7 6 5 4 3 2 1

Publications by BOA Editions, Ltd.—
a not-for-profit corporation under section 501 (c) (3)
of the United States Internal Revenue Code—
are made possible with the assistance of grants from
the Literature Program of the New York State Council on the Arts,
the Literature Program of the National Endowment for the Arts,
the Sonia Raiziss Giop Charitable Foundation,
the Lannan Foundation,
as well as from the Mary S. Mulligan Charitable Trust,
the County of Monroe, NY,
Ames-Amzalak Memorial Trust,
The CIRE Foundation,
and The Rochester Area Community Foundation.

See the Colophon on page 80 for special individual acknowledgments.

Cover Design: Daphne Poulin-Stofer
Cover Art: "Sculptural Group (table group) of Two Griffins Attacking a Fallen Doe,"
    courtesy of The J. Paul Getty Museum.
Interior Design and Composition: Richard Foerster
Manufacturing: McNaughton & Gunn
BOA Logo: Mirko

LIBRARY OF CONGRESS CATALOGING-IN-PUBLICATION DATA

Kelly, Brigit Pegeen, 1951–
  The orchard : poems / by Brigit Pegeen Kelly.— 1st ed.
    p. cm. — (American poets continuum series ; v. 82)
  ISBN 1-929918-48-8 (pbk. : alk. paper)
  I. Title. II. Series.

PS3561.E3927O73 2004
811'.54—dc22

                                                         2004001483

NATIONAL
ENDOWMENT
FOR THE ARTS

State of the Arts
NYSCA

BOA Editions, Ltd.
Thom Ward, Editor
H. Allen Spencer, Chair
A. Poulin, Jr., President & Founder (1976–1996)
260 East Avenue, Rochester, NY 14604
www.boaeditions.org

Contents

I

Black Swan : 11

Blessed Is the Field : 13

The Garden of the Trumpet Tree : 15

Blacklegs : 17

The Wolf : 19

Brightness from the North : 20

Sheep Child : 22

The South Gate : 24

Sheet Music : 25

II

The Satyr's Heart : 29

Two Boys : 30

Rose of Sharon : 32

Windfall : 33

Midwinter : 35

Elegy : 37

Pale Rider : 39

Masque : 43

III

The Dragon : 47

The Foreskin : 48

The Orchard : 49

Plants Fed On by Fawns : 53

Lion : 55

The Dance : 57

The Rain's Consort : 60

IV

The Sparrow's Gate : 65

Acknowledgments : 73

About the Author : 75

Colophon : 80

for Maria

I

Black Swan

I told the boy I found him under a bush.
What was the harm? I told him he was sleeping
And that a black swan slept beside him,
The swan's feathers hot, the scent of the hot feathers
And of the bush's hot white flowers
As rank and sweet as the stewed milk of a goat.
The bush was in a strange garden, a place
So old it seemed to exist outside of time.
In one spot, great stone steps leading nowhere.
In another, statues of horsemen posting giant stone horses
Along a high wall. And here, were triangular beds
Of flowers flush with red flowers. And there,
Circular beds flush with white. And in every bush
And bed flew small birds and the cries of small birds.
I told the boy I looked for him a long time
And when I found him I watched him sleeping,
His arm around the swan's moist neck,
The swan's head tucked fast behind the boy's back,
The feathered breast and the bare breast breathing as one,
And then very swiftly and without making a sound,
So that I would not wake the sleeping bird,
I picked the boy up and slipped him into my belly,
The way one might slip something stolen
Into a purse. And brought him here....
And so it was. And so it was. A child with skin
So white it was not like the skin of a boy at all,
But like the skin of a newborn rabbit, or like the skin
Of a lily, pulseless and thin. And a giant bird
With burning feathers. And beyond them both
A pond of incredible blackness, overarched
With ancient trees and patterned with shifting shades,
The small wind in the branches making a sound

Like the knocking of a thousand wooden bells....
Things of such beauty. But still I might
Have forgotten, had not the boy, who stands now
To my waist, his hair a cap of shining feathers,
Come to me today weeping because some older boys
Had taunted him and torn his new coat,
Had he not, when I bent my head to his head,
Said softly, but with great anger, "I wish I had never
Been born. I wish I were back under the bush,"
Which made the old garden rise up again,
Shadowed and more strange. Small birds
Running fast and the grapple of chill coming on.
There was the pond, half-circled with trees. And there
The flowerless bush. But there was no swan.
There was no black swan. And beneath
The sound of the wind, I could hear, dark and low,
The giant stone hooves of the horses,
Striking and striking the hardening ground.

~~~

Blessed Is the Field

In the late heat the snakeroot and goldenrod run high,
White and gold, the steaming flowers, green and gold,
The acid-bitten leaves....It is good to say first

An invocation. Though the words do not always
Seem to work. Still, one must try. Bow your head.
Cross your arms. Say: *Blessed is the day. And the one*

Who destroys the day. Blessed is this ring of fire
In which we live....How bitter the burning leaves.
How bitter and sweet. How bitter and sweet the sound

Of the single gold and black insect repeating
Its two lonely notes. The insect's song both magnifies
The field and casts a shadow over it, the way

A doorbell ringing through an abandoned house
Makes the falling rooms, papered with lilies and roses
And two-headed goats, seem larger and more ghostly.

The high grasses spill their seed. It is hard to know
The right way in or out. But here, you can have
Which flower you like, though there are not many left,

Lady's thumb in the gravel by the wood's fringe
And on the shale spit beneath the black walnut that houses
The crow, the peculiar cat's-paw, sweet everlasting,

Unbearably soft. Do not mind the crow's bark.
He is fierce and solitary, but he will let us pass,
Patron of the lost and broken-spirited. Behind him

In the quarter ring of sumacs, flagged like circus tents,
The deer I follow, and that even now are watching us,
Sleep at night their restless sleep. I find their droppings

In the morning. And here at my feet is the self-heal,
Humblest of flowers, bloomless but still intact. I ate
Some whole once and did not get well but it may strike

Your fancy. The smell of burning rubber is from
A rabbit carcass the dog dragged into the ravine.
And the smell of lemon is the snakeroot I am crushing

Between my thumb and forefinger....There could be
Beneath this field an underground river full
Of sweet liquid. A dowser might find it with his witching

Wand and his prayers. Some prayers can move
Even the stubborn dirt....Do you hear? The bird
I have never seen is back. Each day at this time

He takes up his ominous clucking, fretting like a baby,
Lonely sweetling. It is hard to know the right way
In or out. But look, the goldenrod is the color

Of beaten skin. Say: *Blessed are those who stand still
In their confusion. Blessed is the field as it burns.*

The Garden of the Trumpet Tree

Someone stuck an apple in the stone head's open mouth. A grave insult. But I did not take it out. Maybe a boy did it, running through the gardens at night, his pockets full of fruit. Or maybe it was a ghost bored with its lot. It does not matter. Today I stood for the first time before the bodiless head and the strange flowering tree it guards. I tried not to laugh. The head on its post stood no taller than I. The head that had bullied me for so long, the great stone head that only the darkness had been able to silence, bagging it each night with a soft cloth sack, the way the heads of those to be hanged are bagged, made no sound. I tried not to think: This is your just dessert: Pillar of pride, pilloried. I touched with both hands the eyes of the head the way a blind person might. They were huge and swollen like the eyes of the deaf composer, or the eyes of the mad poet who left his wife alone while he spent his days in paradise. I touched with one finger the warm fruit. Against the pale cast of the stone the apple shone uncommonly bright, and behind it the thousand and thousand blossoms of the trumpet tree shone uncommonly bright. The fruit and the blossoms were the same scarlet color, and I could see for the first time in the yellow morning light the curious tree for what it was. Not a tree in flower, as I had so long thought, but a flowerless tree coupled with a blossoming trumpet vine. The vine had grown snakelike up and around the trunk, and it had grown so large it had half-strangled the small tree, crawling over every branch and shoot, until the vine and the tree were almost indistinguishable, green flesh and charred wood, flowers and rot, a new creation, a trumpet tree, tree out of time, the smoldering center of some medieval dream. The flowers swam forward in the light, each scarlet bloom so intricate and unlikely—downswung, fluted, narrower than the narrowest piping, forked with yellow silk—it looked as if it had been sewn by hand, the whole improbable tree looked as if it had been worked with impossible patience by a woman's pale hands. Bees stumbled in and out, shaking the flowers. From nowhere a hummingbird appeared, iridescent, green, flipping its shining tail, a creature more fish than bird, more insect than fish, spinning and sipping. To nowhere it returned. The garden stood perfectly still. And for a moment in that garden it seemed as if sound and silence were the same thing, for a moment it seemed as if the thousand and thousand tiny trumpets were blowing a thousand and thousand shining notes, blown glass notes, the liquid substance of the air itself, glass and fire, the morning flushed to perfect fullness. I stood for a long time, breathing in the strange perfume of those scentless flowers. I thought of how the crow would come in an hour or two and plant his dusty feet on the carved head and pluck the fruit apart, piece by sweetened piece. I looked at the blossoming tree. I looked at the stone head. I touched the warm fruit. And I took the apple out. There was no sound. It was like closing the eyes of the dead.

Blacklegs

The sheep has nipples, the boy said,
And fur all around. The sheep
Has black legs, his name is Blacklegs,
And a cry like breaking glass.
The glass is broken. The glass
Is broken, and the milk falls down.

The bee has a suffering softness,
The boy said, a ring of fur,
Like a ring of fire. He burns
The flowers he enters, the way
The rain burns the grass. The bee
Has six legs, six strong legs,
And when he flies, the legs
Whistle like a blade of grass
Brought to the lips and blown.

The boy said, The horse runs hard
As sorrow, or a storm, or a man
With a stolen purse in his shirt.
The horse's legs are a hundred
Or more, too many to count,
And he holds a moon white as fleece
In his mouth, cups it like water
So it will not spill out.

And the boy said this. I am a boy
And a man. My legs are two,
And they shine black as the arrows
That drop down on my throat
And my chest to draw out the blood
The bright animals feed on,

Those with wings, those without,
The ghosts of the heart—whose
Hunger is a dress for my song.

~~~

The Wolf

The diseased dog lowered her head as I came close, as if to make
Of her head a shadow, something the next few hours
Would erase, swiftly, something of no account. And what came
To mind was the she-wolf, beneath the wild fig, nursing
The boys who would build what amounted to a lasting city
On this earth. And it was as if, on that hot afternoon, I was standing
Not in the empty aisle between the gardens, that have been
Reduced to nothing except the most rudimentary plants
And the eroding outlines of brick walls and barren terraces,
But in the white light of a studio, in which a sculptor,
Working from the only model he has, a poor dog, is carving
Out of the blackest of black stones a female wolf with two rows
Of triangular tits, which look like the twin rows of cedars the dog
Swam through and from which two boys are suspended,
Fat-thighed and fated. And the truth is both dog and wolf
Are ancient, for the sick dog comes not from the garden
But from another time, in another city, a sabbath day, foreign,
The street completely empty, the day shapely around me,
The houses, the walks, all ordered and white; and then
Out of the ordered whiteness proceeds a thing of great disorder,
A shape from the world of shadows, something to drive
Away. But I did not drive her away, though I could do
Nothing for her. And now I would make of her something
Better than she could make of herself—though the wolf
Is only remembered in her prime, and not as she must
Have been years later, after all that would pass had passed.

Brightness from the North

Bright shapes in the dark garden, the gardenless stretch
Of old yard, sweetened now by the half-light
As if by burning flowers. Overture. First gesture.
But not even that, the pause before the gesture,
The window frame composing the space, so it
Seems as if time has stopped, as if this half-dark,
This winter grass, plated with frost, these unseen
Silent birds might stay forever. It seems as if
This might be what forever is, the presence of time
Overriding the body of time, the fullness of time
Not a moment but a being, watchful and unguarded,
Unguarded and gravely watched this garden—
The black fir with its long aristocratic broken branches,
The cluster of three tiny tipped arborvitae
Damp as sea sponges, the ghostly sycamore shedding
Its skin, and the sweet row of yews along the walk
Into which people throw their glittering trash....
And who, when the light rises, will come up the walk?
We can say no one will come—the day will be empty
Because you are no longer in it. We can say
The things of the day do not fill it. We can say
The eye is not filled by seeing. Nor silenced
By blinding. We can say, we can say your body
Appeared on the table, and swiftly disappeared—
Do not let the sun go down on the dead figure,
Do not fix the dead figure in mind, the false face,
Remember as you should remember, by heart,
In the garden's dark chamber—and the ground
Took the body, and the ground was pleased.
And oh, now, the busy light comes too quickly,
The gray grass unrolling, birds mewling in the trees,
Dawn raising the walls of day, the rooms we live in,

All our murals, pictures of gardens and presiding deities,
Things painted on plaster to keep the dying company,
A toppled jar, a narrow bird, an ornamental tree
With no name, and crouched beneath the stone table,
The lion with four heads, who looks this morning
As he rises from the shadows, like the creature
Who carries on his back the flat and shining earth.

Sheep Child

I wanted a child. What then, this? The sheep
Stands dumb behind the fence. Stands dumb.
Demanding what? Pity? Affection? A breast full
Of milk? He's up to his neck in his filthy fur.
Honey to the flies. Rancid honey. Each coarse
Curl dipped in it. The flies reeling. A sullen
Moment....Oh, Sheep, Sheep, this is my undoing,
That you have a thought and I would read it. I would
Put my head up to your smelly head and watch
The pretty pictures sliding past: Look! there goes
The flowerless larch, lurching over the ground
Like a skiff. And that black thing spinning in the dung
Is a truck tire stuffed with hay. And here, now,
Down from the elm, comes the crow, bully bird
Beating and beating the air with his wide wings,
As if calling the field to order....There is no order.
What day of the week is this? Wash day?
Bake day? What hour of what day?....Behind you,
Flanked by steely thistle, stands the old goat,
Contemptuous, uninterested, gnawing on the last
Of a Sunday dress; and "I had a goat once,"
The thought that comes to me, "I had a small
Black goat, who pounded his head against a tree
Until he was dead. His name was Bumblebee...."
Well, night is coming on. No, it is dead afternoon.
But there is something about night in this cloud-
Shadowed field. Perhaps the stars are shifting
Behind the veil of day? Perhaps. Perhaps....Oh,
I would turn this pretty. You see the cowbirds
Riding the boney heiffer by the overturned bathtub?
The birds are dung-colored, yes, but when
They rise and swim together they change color,

Brown to red, the way the light changes color
At dusk. And, yes, the swans by the back fence
Are foul-tempered and mean as sin, but look
How their necks wave about now like the stems
Of lilies in the wind....lilies blowing in the wind....
The goat snorts and turns his back. He has
Swallowed the last of the dress....Oh, Sheep, Sheep,
This is my undoing, that you have a thought
And I *can* read it. Dear Monstrous Child, I would
Nurse you if I could. But you are far too large,
And I am far too old for such foolishness.

The South Gate

Light cups the breasts of the lion. Who remains
Unbothered. Stone lion. Stained breasts suddenly
Full of milk. And no one to feed on them. No one
To catch the warm liquid as it falls, sweet and fast,
To the ground. Moss on the lion's legs. Moss
Bloodying her small feet. Moss darkening the fruit trees
Dressed now in the snow that raises the ghosts
Of dead flowers: a visible shadow: a touchable shadow:
Flesh of water and ash. Like the sun, the lion
Is a two-faced creature. One face looks forward.
The other back. One grins. The other grimaces.
Her four eyes are old. *Oh, it is a far, far country*
The lion comes from. A place almost unimaginable,
So dull are we. The lion herself almost unimaginable,
Even with her curious form stationed above us.
Wide the arms of the roses nailed to the wall below her.
Dry the weeds. White the snow dressing the ground
And then dressing it no more. Low the sound
Where no sound should be. Deep in the heart of the ground.
The lion will bear a child. How can a stone lion
Bear a living child? Because still in the corner
Of her deformed head a dream lodges. Her breasts
Produce milk. The sweet milk falls to the ground.
The ground is a flock of dead birds. The wind
Rises. The fed offspring stirs. Soon he will stagger
From burial. Terrible. Wrapped in soiled cloth.
Stinking. Lion flesh and bird flesh and man flesh.
We would prefer this were a trick. Strings
And ropes. But it is not. The lion will grow large.
The greenness is his hunger. His hunger will overtake
The ground and soon devour even the mother.
She will sleep in his belly. He will rock her softly.

Sheet Music

If you cannot trust the dog, the faithful one?
And is this anyway a dog? The shadows move,
Dog and dog, two lanky figures, three, sniffing
The garden's charred terrain, the darkening grass

The bleeding beds of flowers, sniffing the stones
And lunging at the rabbits that spring from the beds,
Wet creatures, mad with haste, mad and wet
And white as the half-hearted moon that stepped

Behind the clouds and has not come back....The rain
Fell hard, and now the mist rises, consolidates, disperses,
That thought, this, your face, mine, the shapes
Complicating the air around the abandoned birdhouse,

Big as a summer hotel, thirty rooms
For thirty birds, thirty perches from which to sing.
Such is the moon when it is full. A giant birdhouse
Tilted high on a steel pole, a pale blue box

Full of the shredded sheet music of long-dead birds....
The dogs move fast. How will I follow? And which one?
They are not in agreement. If the dog cannot be trusted,
Then what? The foot? But the foot is blind, the grass

Cold through the thin socks, the instep bared like a neck.
And now the flowers rise. The mums and asters,
The tall gladioli knocked back as the rain creeps up
In the mist, and the mist thickens and moves about me

Like a band of low-bred mummers, dripping scent,
Pulling my hair, my arms, trying to distract me,

But still I hear it, the dark sound that begins at the edge
Of the mind, at the far edge of the uncut field

Beyond the garden—a low braying, donkey
Or wolf, a low insistent moan. If I whistle
Will the dogs come? Can I gather their trailing leashes
And hold them in my hand? They cannot be held.

How pale the paint of the birdhouse. How ghastly pale
The sound of the cry coming closer....If I forsake
The dogs?....If I forsake the mummers?....If I step
Like a fool into the glassy outer darkness?....*O self*....

II

The Satyr's Heart

Now I rest my head on the satyr's carved chest,
The hollow where the heart would have been, if sandstone
Had a heart, if a headless goat man could have a heart.
His neck rises to a dull point, points upward
To something long gone, elusive, and at his feet
The small flowers swarm, earnest and sweet, a clamor
Of white, a clamor of blue, and black the sweating soil
They breed in....If I sit without moving, how quickly
Things change, birds turning tricks in the trees,
Colorless birds and those with color, the wind fingering
The twigs, and the furred creatures doing whatever
Furred creatures do. So, and so. There is the smell of fruit
And the smell of wet coins. There is the sound of a bird
Crying, and the sound of water that does not move....
If I pick the dead iris? If I wave it above me
Like a flag, a blazoned flag? My fanfare? Little fare
With which I buy my way, making things brave?
No, that is not it. Uncovering what is brave. The way
Now I bend over and with my foot turn up a stone,
And there they are: the armies of pale creatures who
Without cease or doubt sew the sweet sad earth.

Two Boys

The boy drowned in the bog. Not a pretty sight.
Not a pretty end. And it no accident. And him
A stranger in town. Rank the berries in the bushes.
And mute the birds. Not like birds at all.
And afternoon come too soon, and then
Come no longer....*What is the life of a man?*
Or one not even a man? Has it the shape of a bird?
Or a dog? Or an insect dressed in robes of white
And robes of green? And if a life takes its own life?
If a man takes from himself a man? Or a bird
From a bird? Or a dog from a dog? What is
That like? Birds may fall faster than thought,
But a dog is no lamb, it will not easily strangle—
Greenness like fire will not swiftly stamp out....
The boy drowned in the bog. He came from
A long way off to lie down in such sickly water.
Not like water at all. Poor and brown. Not one
Fish in it, not one blind fish. There would
Have been a better time. Or place. Better.
But fate, what is it? Who met the boy
By daylight? And how did he know him? By
What seal on the forehead? Talon or star?
Who said, *Thus far shall you come and no
Farther?* This circle of beaten trees. This ring
Of dark water. Who raised the curtain?
Who prompted the action? Who conceived
It in the first place? What prophet in what
Dark room? Did he weep when he wrote
Down the words? Did he watch till the end,
Or did he leave that for others? And what
Did the flesh smell like when the prophecy
Was sealed? A burned flower? Or ripened fruit?

What sang in the trees before the boy
Lay down or after? A child? Or the light?
Or nothing. Just a bird. Nothing. And then
Night coming on. And morning coming after....
And so we have a story. But still the story
Does not end. Green the cress by the water.
Green the insect's wing. Now the living boy
Finds the dead one. A gift for early rising.
A worm for the bird. The boy did not know
What he saw. He thought the dead boy
Must be something other. Flesh of a lily.
Or a fallen hat. He thought what he thought.
And then he thought no longer. The wind
At once loud in the trees. The birds loud.
The boy had wanted a brother. But this
Was not what he meant. Had he said
The wrong words? *Did words have such power?*
And then he saw what he saw, and he knew
From this day forward, for better or worse,
For worse or better, he would carry this shadow
Of no certain shape—now a lamb, now a bird,
Now a boy dressed as a woman—from here
To there, and there to here. Back to this bog
Or another. This wood or another. Berries
Bright or rank. Water foul or pure. Birds loud
In the trees. Or still. And softer than fleece,
Softer than grass, it already raining.

~~~

Rose of Sharon

I loved the rose of Sharon. I would have loved it
For its name alone. I loved its fleshy blossoms.
How fat they were. How fast they fell. How the doves,
Mean as spit, fought the finches and the sparrows
For the golden seed I spilled beneath the bush.
How I threw seed just to watch the birds fight.
And the blossoms fallen were like watered silk
Loosely bound. And the blossoms budding
Were like the dog's bright penis first emerging
From its hairy sheath. And the blossoms opened wide
Were like the warm air above the pool of Siloam.
Tree of breath. Pink flowers floating on water.
The flushed blossoms themselves like water.
Rising. Falling. The wind kicking up skeins
Of scented foam. High-kicking waves. Or laughing
Dancers. O silly thoughts. But a great sweetness....
And then it was over. An ice storm felled the tree.
With a clean cut, as if with a hatchet. One year
A whole flock of birds. One year a crop of fruit
That melted on the tongue, a kind of manna, light
As honey, just enough to sustain one. And then nothing.
The breasts gone dry. The window opening onto
Bare grass. The small birds on the wire waiting
For the seed I do not throw. *Pride of my heart,*
Rose of Sharon. *Pool of scented breath*. Rose
Of Sharon. How inflated my sorrow. But the tree
Itself was inflated. A perpetual feast. A perpetual
Snowfall of warm confetti....And now I worry.
Did the bush fear the ice? Did it know of the ice's
Black designs? Did its featherweight nature darken
Just before it was felled? Was it capable of darkening?

Windfall

There is a wretched pond in the woods. It lies at the north end of a piece of land owned by a man who was taken to an institution years ago. He was a strange man. I only spoke to him once. You can still find statues of women and stone gods he set up in dark corners of the woods, and sometimes you can find flowers that have survived the collapse of the hidden gardens he planted. Once I found a flower that looked like a human brain growing near a fence, and it took my breath away. And once I found, among some weeds, a lily white as snow....No one tends the land now. The fences have fallen and the deer grown thick, and the pond lies black, the water slowly thickening, the banks tangled with weeds and grasses. But the pond was very old even when I first came upon it. Through the trees I saw the dark water steaming, and smelled something sweet rotting, and then as I got closer, I saw in the dark water shapes, and the shapes were golden, and I thought, without really thinking, that I was looking at the reflections of leaves or of fallen fruit, though there were no fruit trees near the pond and it was not the season for fruit. And then I saw that the shapes were moving, and I thought they moved because I was moving, but when I stood still, still they moved. And still I had trouble seeing. Though the shapes took on weight and muscle and definite form, it took my mind a long time to accept what I saw. The pond was full of ornamental carp, and they were large, larger than the carp I have seen in museum pools, large as trumpets, and so gold they were almost yellow. In circles, wide and small, the plated fish moved, and there were so many of them they could not be counted, though for a long time I tried to count them. And I thought of the man who owned the land standing where I stood. I thought of how years ago in a fit of madness or high faith he must have planted the fish in the pond, and then forgotten them, or been taken from them, but still the fish had grown and still they thrived, until they were many, and their bodies were fast and bright as brass knuckles or cockscombs. I tore pieces of my bread and threw them at the carp, and the carp leaped, as I have not seen carp do before, and they fought each other for the bread, and they were not like fish but like gulls or wolves, biting and leaping. Again and again, I threw the bread. Again and again, the fish leaped and wrestled. And below them, below the leaping fish, near the bottom of the pond, something slowly circled, a giant form that never rose to the bait and never came fully into view, but moved patiently in and out of the murky shadows, out and in. I watched that form, and after the bread was gone and after the golden fish had again grown quiet, my mind at last constructed a shape for it, and I saw for the space of one moment or two with perfect clarity, as if I held the heavy creature in my hands, the tarnished body of an ancient carp. A thing both fragrant and foul. A lily and a man's brain bound together in one body. And then the fish was gone. He turned and the shadows closed around him. The water grew blacker, and the steam rose from it, and the golden carp held still, still uncountable. And softly they burned, themselves like flowers, or like fruit blown down in an abandoned garden.

～

Midwinter

And again, at dusk, I find the madwoman,
Crouched on the stone bridge by the cornfields,
Feeding corn to the fish. Though there are no fish

In the river. The river is dead or nearly so,
The water gray as stolen sleep or spoiled sheets.
The woman looks sheepish. But not like a sheep.

Her skin is sallow. Her hair uncombed. Her coat
Unravelling at wrist and hem. The coat's woven cloth
Has faded from overwashing and it is the same color

As the haze the fields exude in the morning or sometimes
At dusk, a foggy lavender mist that smells of tin
And fresh blood and of the slender green sticks we burn

When we strip back the garden in the first warm weather....
Not like a sheep. More like a child who has gotten
The sum wrong, but stubbornly knows the sum

Doesn't matter as much as one thinks....Corn cobs
Drop into the poisoned water. The ghostly cobs
Float and turn like boats made from paper. And the day

Grows colder....When the woman speaks she does not
Look up. She does not take her eyes from the sliding water.
"Feed the fish?" she asks. And then she shudders.

Frightened, perhaps, as I am by the flat sound of her voice.
Or by the sudden thinning of the air. Or by the way
The narrow rim of light over the blackened tree line

Comes and is gone before one has time to see it....
If I say, "We can go home now," if I kneel down
And say, "We can go home, the fish are sleeping,"

To *whom* do I speak? And out of *what* knowledge?...
The water moves like ash. And like ash it makes
No sound. The woman crouched on the stone bridge

Picks from the corn heaped at her feet one pale cob,
And without looking up, she holds it out toward me.

Elegy

Wind buffs the waterstained stone cupids and shakes
Old rain from the pines' low branches, small change
Spilling over the graves the years have smashed
With a hammer—*forget this, forget that, leave no*
Stone unturned. The grass grows high, sweet-smelling,
Many-footed, ever-running. No one tends it. No
One comes....*And where am I now?*....Is this a beginning,
A middle, or an end?....Before I knew you I stood
In this place. Now I forsake the past as I knew it
To feed you into it. But that is not right. You *step*
Into it. I *find* you here, in the shifting grass,
In the late light, as if you had always been here.
Behind you two torn black cedars flame white
Against the darkening fields....If you turn to me,
Quiet man? If you turn? If I speak softly?
If I say, *Take off, take off your glasses....Let me see*
Your sightless eyes?....I will be beautiful then....
Look, the heart moves as the moths do, scuttering
Like a child's thoughts above this broken stone
And that. And I lie down. I lie down in the long grass,
Something I am not given to doing, and I feel
The weight of your hand on my belly, and the wind
Parts the grasses, and the distance spills through—
The glassy fields, the black black earth, the pale air
Streaming headlong toward the abbey's far stones
And streaming back again....The drowned scent of lilacs
By the abbey, it is a drug. It drives one senseless.
It drives one blind. You can cup the enormous lilac cones
In your hands—ripened, weightless, and taut—
And it is like holding someone's heart in your hands,
Or holding a cloud of moths. I lift them up, my hands.
Grave man, bend toward me. Lay your face....*here*....

Rest....I took the stalks of the dead wisteria
From the glass jar propped against the open grave
And put in the shell-shaped yellow wildflowers
I picked along the road. I cannot name them.
Bread and butter, perhaps. I am not good
With names. But nameless you walked toward me
And I knew you, a swelling in the heart,
A silence in the heart, the wild wind-blown grass
Burning—as the sun falls below the earth—
Brighter than a bed of lilies struck by snow.

~~~

Pale Rider

I found her beneath the fruiting honeysuckle,
The fallen doe. The hunter had cut her legs off,
And because the doe was so small, killed out of season,
The leg wounds looked huge, like neck wounds.
I found her in summer and then I forgot about her.
But many months later, on a day of cold rain,
And then unfallen snow, when I was tired because
I had not slept, and because I was tired, anxious,
I walked back to the grotto in the oldest part of the woods.
It is a dark unsettling place and I am drawn to it.
No sun finds its way through the trees, even in winter,
And, as if the place were cursed, birds pass through
Quickly or not at all, and they will not sing. Dusk
Had come early. The steep hill rose up black
Above the cave's blue walls, and from the water
Pooled on the rocks, the mist was already rising.
I could feel it before I saw it, stirring like the clouds
Of insects that sift through the swales in summer.
And then the mist took on weight and turned silver.
And then it grew heavier still and turned white.
I was having trouble seeing. I heard the call of a night bird,
Far off, perishable, and from the branches, high
And low, water dripped, a dull repeating sound,
Like the sound of many mute people flicking one
Finger slow and hard against their palms. And then
The sound fell off, and the cold mist turned warm,
As if it were coming not from the pools of water
But from deep within the ground, and in the mist
I smelled flowers. And I was confused. I thought
For a moment it must be summer and not winter,
And that I would see, if the mist suddenly thinned,
Not a stripped thorn, clinging to the grotto's rim,

But a blooming honeysuckle bush. I could taste
The honeysuckle on my tongue, a taste that was faint
At first, slightly rancid. But as the mist grew thicker
And thicker, golden now, softly vibrating, the taste
Grew stronger, and more sweet, like the taste of ether,
Until it seemed as if I were standing in a cloud,
Or a hive. I looked up: whiteness, milky, lit from within,
And, like mother-of-pearl, *something*, not clear, a shape,
The shape of an owl or a snowy hawk, hanging
Perfectly still, the way a hawk will hang for hours
In a stiff wind, but there was no wind. And the shape
Was not an owl, nor a hawk, but a shape my mind
At first resisted, the way my mind sometimes refuses
To make sense of words that are perfectly clear,
Simple words, spoken slowly and with great care,
Because the words are so improbable, or will tell me,
Good or bad, the thing I most wish not to hear,
"He is dead," say, or, "Take up your bed and walk."
Below that shape I stood, a pointed shape, golden,
Not a hawk, nor a boot, nor a silk hat made of mist
Yet still somehow indistinguishable from the mist,
But something else, until my mind gave in to my eyes,
And the thing I had not wanted to see, or thought
I could not see, hung suspended above me, a face,
The head on its long neck of the doe I had found
Beneath the honeysuckle—such a frail creature,
Too small to have been killed, so small the hunter
Could have carried her home on his back had he so desired,
But he had not so desired. And I knew it was *that* doe,
Though I cannot say how I knew, her narrow face small
And dark and shining, until the mist closed over it,
And it was gone. And then, almost at once, the face
Appeared in another place, and again the mist closed,
And again the face came back, as in a game,
Until I saw that the face was not one but two,
Not two faces, but four, a flock of small deer, but no,

Not a flock, and again my mind refused the shape
Taking on weight above me, four heads on four long necks,
Attached to one legless body, one golden swollen body
That smelled of fallen fruit splitting in the sun and shone
The way an image from a dream will darkly shine,
Floating up from childhood, a hand holding out
A piece of torn bread that turns for no reason
Into a block of honeycomb filled not with honey
But with a marbled black and red substance,
Dense and sweet as charred flesh. She shone
The doe, her four heads, held high and perfectly still,
Facing in four different directions. And then I saw
Something else, darker, protruding from her breast.
It was a fifth neck and head, hanging upside down
In front, like the useless third leg of Siamese twins
Joined at the torso that hangs out of the spine,
And is amputated at birth, or like the water-darkened
Rudder of a ship. I heard the hot air sucking in and out
Of the doe's many nostrils, in and out. The mist
Grew darker, and I felt afraid, for I knew even before
My eyes confirmed it, that the fifth head was not
The doe's head at all, as I had thought, but the head
Of a grown child that the doe was trying to deliver
From her breast, and I knew that the child would never
Be born, but must ride always with her, his body
Embedded in hers, his head up to the sky. I wanted
To reach up and touch that head. But I did not do so.
I kept thinking that the doe would disappear, or that
She would say something, that her four mouths, five,
Would open and she would speak, but she did not disappear,
And she did not speak. A doe will never speak.
She will bark or cry out like a child if alarmed, but she
Will not speak. The mist smelled of warm milk,
And the doe's muteness grew loud, and louder still,
Until it was as dizzying as the sound of many trumpets
Blowing a single everlasting note. And I thought

Of the tongue, of how it is a wound, a pool of blood,
And of how you should bind a wound. And I thought
Of the earth covered with poor forked creatures
Walking around with broken faces, their substance
Pouring out in the form of words. And I thought of how
The mist would thicken further until it thinned,
All at once, to nothing, in the night air that smelled
Of sewage and poor man's roses, and of how the sound
Of the water dripping from the trees would return,
Tinnier, less insistent, as the water grew colder.
And I knew that soon on the high hill above the grotto
The fine dry snow would start to fall, and the field
Would draw silence to itself, and then as the air
Grew soft, the dry snow would turn to wet snow,
And the wet snow would lie heavy against the earth,
And the silence would multiply, a dark mass of pulp
And wings stirring above a darker bed, until nothing
Was recognizable to itself, and things were as if dead,
Wrapped in sheets and soaked in spices and oil, and death
A great mercy. And the snow seemed to hiss softly,
Or the falling mist hissed softly, or the water sliding
Down the stones, and the doe's form became more ghostly—
Pale rider, lost in the woods where I was lost. And I stood
In the dark until I closed my eyes. And then I stood no more.

Masque

My foot bleeds on the rocks
Of the shallow stream. The crows
Thick above me and at their backs
The larger gravebirds. This
Is a mean task, this business
Of burying oneself before one
Is dead. The shovel always
Breaks, the weather worsens,
The spot chosen proves to be
The wrong spot, and the words,
The words of mercy one must
Mutter, possess no mercy
For the flesh: *Not with peace,*
Not with peace but with a sword
Is the flesh stripped back,
Its many masks flayed off,
Each mask more extravagant
Than the last, like Bartholomew's
Beautiful and deadly hats,
No end in sight, no fair sight
Of the bared head, the bare stage
Upon whose wooden boards
We must play with passion
Our two parts: Lazarus undone
And that goodfellow Christ.
Hardfellow Christ. *Oh do not lose*
Faith. Work it out. Work it out.
The chief crow performs with panache
His task as smart backdrop
For the naked body dishing dirt
With a broken spade. Brokered wings
And a beaten heart. Dear God! to be

More than a light-hearted jest,
Or a hard-hearted jest. My crow,
My lark, my winsome wren,
My chough, oh sweet-lipped one
Who keeps me to a task
I do not want, let me be more
Than a dove-witted fool. The light
Strikes down between the trees.
The shovel strikes dirt. If the seam
Is good. If the seam is good. Then
The heart will put on for a moment
Its royal robes and become a grave man
Standing before an open crypt
With an air of such command
The stained burial wrappings
Of one much loved, and maligned,
And many days dead, will drop
Away. The self step blind
From its watery grave. And there
Will be: No time. Nor crow.
Nor Lazarus. Nor Christ.
Nor the hand that writes this.

III

The Dragon

The bees came out of the junipers, two small swarms
The size of melons; and golden, too, like melons,
They hung next to each other, at the height of a deer's breast,
Above the wet black compost. And because
The light was very bright it was hard to see them,
And harder still to see what hung between them.
A snake hung between them. The bees held up a snake,
Lifting each side of his narrow neck, just below
The pointed head, and in this way, very slowly
They carried the snake through the garden,
The snake's long body hanging down, its tail dragging
The ground, as if the creature were a criminal
Being escorted to execution or a child king
To the throne. I kept thinking the snake
Might be a hose, held by two ghostly hands,
But the snake was a snake, his body green as the grass
His tail divided, his skin oiled, the way the male member
Is oiled by the female's juices, the greenness overbright,
The bees gold, the winged serpent moving silently
Through the air. There was something deadly in it,
Or already dead. Something beyond the report
Of beauty. I laid my face against my arm, and there
It stayed for the length of time it takes two swarms
Of bees to carry a snake through a wide garden,
Past a sleeping swan, past the dead roses nailed
To the wall, past the small pond. And when
I looked up the bees and the snake were gone,
But the garden smelled of broken fruit, and across
The grass a shadow lay for which there was no source,
A narrow plinth dividing the garden, and the air
Was like the air after a fire, or the air before a storm,
Ungodly still, but full of dark shapes turning.

The Foreskin

I planted the little curl of skin under the magnolia. For a long time I could not remember the name for it, because though I had heard the word and its definition many times, when confronted with the tiny curl of flesh, the word did not seem to resemble the thing I held in hand, as words so often do not resemble the things they represent, or what we imagine them to represent; words can even destroy in their saying the very thing for which they stand. The little curl was pinkish, like an overbred white rabbit's eyes, and yellowing white, like the petals of the magnolia blooms, and a soft blue; and it had a crust of red, for no one had washed it, those who might have done so unprepared for the request for it, so they handed it over in its sullied form, which made it, I thought, more beautiful. And then I did not know what to do with it, for it seemed of great value to me, the purest portion of the man-child's pleasure returned to god, so that the small rain of god might overshadow the rest of his pleasure, make a fertile field of it; and it seemed that the pain, too, the boy had felt when the knife peeled the portion away, and the pain of the one watching, who was afraid to follow the ancient covenants and afraid not to, were folded into this piece of flesh. So I planted it in the black dirt at the crest of the field, and then I planted the magnolia over it. That was the order, first the little petal, now dried, and then the new bush, and in one year or two the bush made blossoms that began as furred buds, like the budding horns of young deer, and turned into large flowers that seemed to have been pieced together with curls of flesh, but magnified, as if under glass, magnified and made dazzling by the sun.

The Orchard

I saw the dog in a dream. Huge white
Boney creature. Big as a horse. At first
I thought it was a horse. It was feeding
On apples. As a horse might. Though not
With a horse's patience. For it was starving.
Its hipbones were empty bowls. The horse
Wolfed down the apples. Without breathing.
Without looking up. The way a dog wolfs
Down meat. And then it growled. And I saw
That the horse *was* a dog. But the apples
Were still apples. Windfall from the orchard
Above the lake. Pitiful place. The few trees
There grow black and yellow. And the thin grasses
Stagger down to the abandoned north field,
Which floods in winter and then freezes—
Blue ground, marbled with red and white,
Like a slab of meat—and when the far deer
Cross over it, and the birds cross over it,
It is as if the memories held within
The meat were rising from it. Or it is like
Flies crawling....I saw the dog in a dream.
And then, days later, just before dawn,
I climbed to the orchard. And there he was.
The same dog. Chewing on a dead doe.
And it was troubling. I thought I might
Still be dreaming—as was the case
When for many months I could not sleep
And I lost the power to tell the figures
In my dreams from those we call real.
I thought the scene might have been staged
For me. By my mind. Or by someone
Who could read my mind. Someone

Who was having a good laugh
At my expense. Or testing me
In some way I could not understand.
Beneath the black and yellow trees,
The dog's skin seemed abnormally white.
And the blood on his broad muzzle shone
Like wet paint. I closed my eyes. Not because
The ghostly creature was now biting
At the neck of the doe, the way
Those dark creatures who drink blood
And live forever do—since the river
Of blood flows forever, the streams
Of an eternal city, forever running,
Forever carrying their musky loads
Of blooming and expiring words
And figures, a thousand thousand
Yellow lights forever flickering off
And on in the black liquid, gold,
Sweet liquid, fallen—I closed my eyes.
Not out of distaste. But to see if the dog
Would disappear, the way the mist
Had thinned and vanished as I climbed
The hill. But the dog was still there
When I opened them. Staring straight at me.
He lifted his large paw. Placed it
On the doe's chest, and started to rip
At her belly. There was the sound
Of cloth tearing. And what did I do?
I picked up an apple. I wanted to see
If the dog—when the apple struck his side
And he fell—would rise in a second form,
And then a third. As dream figures do.
Dog. To horse. To man. Or I wanted to see
If the apple would pass through the dog
As through a ghost. And if the dog
Like the best of ghosts would turn

And instruct me in my confusion.
Or I wanted to bring the scene down
To size. The way the bright lights
That clank on at the end of the play
Show the mad king to be nothing
But a skinny man holding a costume
Of cloth and paste. I wanted the dog
To be just a stray, gnawing on a bone.
Or maybe I wanted none of these things.
Maybe I wanted what the hunter
Wanted when he struck the doe. Maybe
I wanted a piece of the dog's feasting,
The way the hunter wanted a piece
Of the doe's improbable swiftness.
The gun fires. The smell of burnt powder
Sprays up. A knotted string of birds
Unspools across the white sky. And deep
In running blood the hunter thrusts his hands.
I wanted something. But I did not throw
The apple. It was a small fruit. The size
Of a child's hand. Black and yellow. Riddled
With worms and misshapen. I put my teeth
To it. I took a bite. Chill flesh. Rank.
The dog kept feeding. I was not bothered
By the blood. The last of the red leaves
Scudded about me. And a few drops fell
From the dark sky. There is blood
Everywhere. The trees shed it. The sky.
There is no end. And isn't it pretty?
We say. Isn't it pretty? Amn't I?
Isn't the starving dog? Isn't the doe,
Even half-eaten? She gave her body
To the dog. The fallen body looked
So heavy. It looked as if it weighed
Ten thousand pounds. More than the lake
Or the frozen field. The doe dreamed

Of her death and it came to pass.
She courted the hunter and he shot her.
And she fell. And then the man stood
Over her. A white shadow. Laughing.
And then the dog stood over her. A black
Shadow. Laughing. And the dog came close.
The way a lover might. Had the doe
Been human. And he put her mouth to her.
As a lover might. Had he been human.
And her chastened flesh was a chalice.
And she was peaceful. And there was bliss
In this. And some horror. Around her
The thorns shone black and yellow.
And the fallen fruit lay black and yellow.
And black and yellow are the colors
Of the orchard's hive when it masses
And the queen in a fiery constellation
Is carried to new quarters. The wind
Stirred in the orchard. The dog bit
Into the doe's chest. And the apple
In my hand, against my lips, small,
Misshapen, the size of a child's fist,
Full of worms, turned suddenly warm
And soft. And it was as if, on that hill,
While the dog fed and the lake lay
Frozen, I was holding in my hand,
Against my lips, not a piece of fruit,
Not a piece of bitter, half-eaten fruit,
But the still warm and almost beating
Heart of some holy being—just lifted
From the dead body. And the heart
Was heavy. And wet. And it smelled
As it would smell forever. Of myrrh.
And burning blood. And gold.

Plants Fed On by Fawns

All the flowers: the pleated leaves of the hellebore;
And the false blossom of the calla, a leaf like a petal—
The white flesh of a woman bathing—a leaf over-
Shadowing the small flowers hidden in the spadix;
And fly poison, tender little flower, whose cursed root
Pounded into a fine white powder will destroy flies.
But why kill flies? They do not trouble me. They
Are like the fruit the birds feed on. They are like
The wind in the trees, or the sap that threads all things,
The blue blood moving through branch and vine,
Through the wings of dead things and living things....
If I lift my hand? If I write to you? The letters
Can be stored in a box. Can they constitute the shape
Of a love? Can the paper be ground? Can the box
Be altar and garden plot and bed? Can there rise
From the bed the form of a two-headed creature,
A figure that looks both forward and back, keeping
Watch always, one head sleeping while the other wakes,
The bird head sleeping while the lion head wakes,
And then the changing of the guard?....No,
The flies do not trouble me. They are like the stars
At night. Common and beautiful. They are like
My thoughts. I stood at midnight in the orchard.
There were so many stars, and yet the stars,
The very blackness of the night, though perfectly
Cold and clear, seemed to me to be insubstantial,
The whole veil of things seemed less substantial
Than the thing that moved in the dark behind me,
An unseen bird or beast, something shifting in its sleep,
Half-singing and then forgetting it was singing:
Be thou always ravished by love, starlight running
Down and pulling back the veil of the heart,

And then the water that does not exist opening up
Before one, dark as wine, and the unveiled figure
Of the self stepping unclothed, sweetly stripped
Of its leaf, into starlight and the shadow of night,
The cold water warm around the narrow ankles,
The body at its most weightless, a thing so durable
It will—like the carved stone figures holding up
The temple roof—stand and remember its gods
Long after those gods have been forsaken.

~

Lion

It is a hollow affair. You understand. And it has four heads. But this is misleading. Because it has four chests as well and four torsos, and four front legs, which must be hard to understand, since it seems there should be eight, but it has four, and the four front legs are twice the size of a normal leg, and so are the paws, twice the size of normal paws, and the only thing the heads and legs and torsos and chests have in common is the small of the back, one small back held up by a steel post and shared by the four lions, who by this portion of metal, shaped like an inverted bowl, are made into one lion. You see how difficult this is, so forgive my clumsiness. The lion has four heads and he is made of hollowed steel, and I'm sure I could make a song of this if I wanted to, but at the moment I do not feel that cheerful. Hollow, like armor, the lion, like a thing to be worn, not a thing in its own right, except in a museum, of course, where things which are part of a bigger picture are pulled away from that picture and made to stand outside of time, all alone, apart from their given function and the things to which they were born: they stand and stand so that we can stare at them until the mind goes blank, if it were not blank before, which well it might have been. Of hollow steel the lion is made, and his handsome heads, his four rusted heads—the old gold paint now flaking as if the lion had mange or leprosy—oh poor creature—are both hollow and flat on top, as if the crowns of the heads had been cut clean off in an experiment, or a massacre; but they were not, the heads were crownless from birth, fashioned to hold high the slate table top stolen from the mansion that burned. This is true. And they do. The mansion burned, the slate was stolen, and the lion's four heads holding up the heavy stone table are flat and hollow. But how handsome the faces, bearded like pharoahs, and how beautiful the forelocks, like Elvis curls, and how high-boned and fine the cheeks, and how proud and furious the pulling of these lions below the table top, and above the cement cracked by weeds, and beside the overgrown garden, this pulling and pulling in four different directions, as if the lions were the four winds of the world yoked together, or the four guardians of the four regions—so that if you look at them long enough, look at the lions, pulling so hard, trying to get somewhere, they seem to spin in a wheel, and it is a fiery wheel they spin in, as if the sun itself that spins through the heavens had been cut loose and were doing a wild dance here in this little yard, a mad dance, a sweet disfigured dance that cannot be deciphered, but still delights, as such things on some days delight.

The Dance

She was so sick, a pathetic dog, ugly as sin, and wild, a blond bitch,
Who seemed to be old, her fur going white, though that was probably
Part of the sickness. And she looked as if she had just given birth,
Because her dugs were swollen, but they were also disfigured,
So maybe they were full of rot and not milk, and her gait was uneven,
Her head down and swinging, causing her to list in half circles
From which she had to turn back. And it was painful to watch
Her work her way up the stone path, in and out of the black shadows
Cast by the imported cypresses. In she walked. Out she walked.
That is how things go. But that is not how this went. For when
The dog came to the circle of stone surrounding the stone pillar
The beautiful man stood on, bent over and sideways across one knee,
His huge genitals pushed forward, she stopped. And at his feet,
She struggled down to her knees, the way a newborn calf struggles
Up to his feet, her hindquarters in the air, and then she opened
Her mouth wide, and turning her head to the side, as if her ear hurt,
She began to bring something up. I thought it might be
The sickness itself, a dark swollen mass with hair on it, but it
Kept coming, the way a child comes, a raised fist, and soon a head,
Not a child's but a man's, lay smashed against the dirt and stones,
And the dog's poor mouth seemed broken, and then broken
Further as a blunt shoulder shoved free, and then an arm,
The wretched body of the dog, if it could be called that, body or dog,
A shaking thing, a ghostly thing, like a trembling lilac bush,
Or a snake's lit rattle. I do not know how to describe this. The insects
Had gone dumb. And the newborn man began to wrestle his way
Out of the creature only half his size, unless he were half a man,
But he was not, for after a time, long or short, a full man lay
On his back on the stones, and the dog lay like a castaway coat
To the side, just a shadowy rag of cloth and bone. And then
The stone man bent over, bent to see. As if he had been standing
All these years in the same difficult position, waiting for the waters

Far below to deliver this naked creature, that looked like him,
But smaller, onto these white stones, circling his high pillar,
Circled again by a wall of trimmed privet, the imported cypresses
And their shadows stretching away in four different directions,
Through the gardens of live forever, and the gardens of marigolds,
And the beds of now-dead irises, and the dark domain of the roses,
From which, one day, the gentle marble woman vanished, never
To return, the heat high and stifling, the crow high up in the quiet,
The silence of night awake inside the silence of day—and oh, yes,
It is carried, night a little creature carried by the day, day's child,
A disfigured creature, and then night grown full, and day carried,
A beautiful creature, night's child, a white mewling thing
Like a rose—and then the pale man on the rocks climbed to his feet
And stood for a moment, the way the man above him stood,
And he did something like a little dance, assuming one still
Pose after another, his muscles tight as stones, and the light
Around him laughing ha ha ha ha ha ha, not in amusement
But in deep pleasure, the crow laughing ha ha ha ha ha ha,
And the handsome cypresses spinning like dreidels....Things
Will be fed on. The rose is fed on by blight, a white ghost,
And by beetles, tiny green stones, and the calf dead for a week
Behind the far wall is fed on by vultures, and the bending stone
Statue is fed on by the rain and the wind—they vie for his eyes,
His fruit—and the man dances for this, for the devouring.
Does a cat walk by? Yes, a black cat walks by, delicate, precise,
And the crow laughs ha ha ha ha ha ha. And now the man's time
Is up. The figure on the pillar breathes in and draws back
To his stone state, and the man below sits down and struggles
To pull on the suit of rag and bone, the man growing smaller
As the suit grows larger, the dog's mouth at last closing over
The crown of the man's head, and the poor dog laboring
To her feet, and beginning again her slow walk, up and on,
In and out of the shadows, her head swinging from side to side,
As if she were divining for water. She will walk all the way
Around the world, until she comes back to the circle of stone,
And the dance is repeated. Again and again, she will do this,

Until the game is over, and on some days, when the heat
Is a ghastly flower, someone may, for a moment, see her.

The Rain's Consort

So, the lion, so his stiff wings, so the black moss that stains
Both his mouth and his wings, moss the color of fruit blood,
Or of pity, pity for the self that labors and labors
And spins only the wind, bride of the wind, oh foolish one.
So, the lion on the post, half-buried in lilacs, and below him
The small retaining pond filled with black water so thick
And still it cannot reflect the lion submerged in lilacs,
Nor the three stone cupids who poke him with their horns
And their harps, mean as vexing sparrows, bright
As low born sparrows, lilacs the color of figs or sparrows,
Or of the rain itself, laughing, and coming, and going.
The cupids' bellies are swollen like the bellies of pregnant
Women or small overbred dogs fed on delicacies. What
Offspring will they bear?—these boys, who torment a lion
In a cloud of lilacs, his single wing struck off near the tip,
And the day now at its center, uncertain of its purpose,
And the pond at its blackest, no bigger than a skirt
Fanned out on the grass, and the small grave caged
Near the pond all pock-marked and shining. Lilacs the color
Of rain, and rain the color of plucked flowers scattering,
Or coins falling on the dirt, and at the base of the lion
A dead sparrow lying open and held in silence as if in a palm,
The bird's feathers easing the skin, the stone lion marking
For a moment the small bird's grave, though the lion
Is no gravestone but the graveyard's guardian, and the rain
Is the sparrow's consort. And now the dead sparrow's
Brother sticks its head in the mouth of the lion, a test
Of courage, beating the boys at their own game, and the name
On the caged grave comes clear, James Herod. King,
Was he, tetrarch, a sparrow like the rest....To the north,
Red sumac shoots rise up like herds of antlered deer,
Or like fences of iron spikes, and near the entrance

A rope, swinging in the wind, hangs from an oak, as a child
Once swung in the wind, grieving for her father, a grief
So pure it still holds the day on its course....Shadowy applause
For the lion. The child singing in the wind. The child
Unclothed. The tarnished silver vines looking dead
Though they are not. Always they break into blossom
And grief....Shadowy applause for the sparrow and the lion.

IV

The Sparrow's Gate

And the bird shot through, who, had the stone arms been intact,
    would have dashed his small brains out and fallen like a bloody
    cloth to the grass—

the bird shot through—

and the absence, the missing arms beneath the beautiful slope of the
    woman's shoulders, her perpetual *at ease*, the woman not
    requiring as the man might the order to relax—

the absence, beneath the beautiful birthright of the woman's
    shoulders, the domes of mosques, or snowy hills, cold
    abundant hills,

    though now all is hot, the air is hot, the grass is hot, the sweet
    stench of stewed greens rising like the savor god feeds on, such
    a lot of flesh to make a pleasing smell, bull flesh, and lamb
    flesh, and dove flesh, all the steaming pools of blood and flies,

    but that was long ago, as the heavy-breasted body, mulled in
    sweat and patience that gave birth beneath the scuptor's hands
    to her giant twin above, stood long ago, a thousand plus a
    thousand years or more;

beneath the beautiful slouch of the woman's shoulder, one shoulder
    to be exact, just where the shoulder and the upper arm meet,
    beside the brimming breast

the bird shot through—

and the absence we had forgotten
    came back;

and it was not, as one might expect, an insult, nor a disfigurement,
   nor a lack;

not the deflowered sun-stricken bush swamping the broken
   fountain, a stone flower thrusting out a long-dead pipe below
   the woman's feet;

not the sparrow's foolhardy bravura that blasted him safely past the
   woman's breast and into the trees, only to impale him soon
   after on the hound's blunt tooth;

not the newborn rabbit outside the gate, ghastly pink, born too late
   and bushwacked by the sudden uprising of the gardener's
   sprinklers that just as quickly dropped back and left the slick
   creature trembling like the mayflies that live for one day only,
   or like a young deer before a storm;

not an incapacity, nor a short-sightedness,
nor a tunneling of vision, the world narrowing down to this alley
   between two rows of rotting trees that leads to a fetid pond,
   screened by narrow grasses and blackened by sludge and a half-
   day's dream;

not the small girl years ago when her arm went numb after she had
   been swung and swung in a circle saying, when her mother
   pressed the mute flesh, It is hiding, it is hiding, Mother,

   (and what, had the arm been taken altogether, would the girl
   have said, *To a far country it has gone, Mother, it is lost and cannot
   find its way back?*);

not the terrible draining at the center of the day when the spirit
   topples like a statue to the grass, or like a woman who has
   given blood and risen too quickly to her narrow feet;

not a shame,

not a word pronounced slowly and then spelled with great care
    letter by letter all wrong into the dark beyond the stage, and
    the following silence that flies back and attaches itself like a
    dark bird to the brain;

not the hound with no sense of smell blundering blindly through
    the woods or lying in the sun with his mouth slung open to
    catch flies and stray birds;

not the flushed bloom of the ripe marigolds pulled up by the
    hundreds and cast onto the gardener's fire so that new flowers
    can be put in and death beaten to the punch, the perfumed
    smoke rising acrid as rotting fur;

not the wind butting its head against the garden wall like the boy
    who long ago killed the bird or tore the cloth,

    nor the remorse of the mother years later when she
    remembers locking the door against him and realizes too late
    that the fabric of the world—the sky itself, the trees, the garden
    and its terrifying colors, the dusky texture of the boy's hair—is
    woven from rebuttals and embraces, takes on its hue, retains its
    shape as surely as the patterns on the loom, to which the
    woman had given too much importance, mistaking cloth for
    flesh;

not the murderous fanfare of the mosquitoes, a visible
    derangement, multiplying over the pond's shallow water;

not the harp dropped into the pond and retrieved years later,
    unstrung and warped beyond recognition, good only for the
    fire, and not much good for that;

not that;

not a single sheet of paper, a letter whose words no matter how
    rearranged are a dark glass held up before the world upon
    which one can rap and rap and get no answer;

not that rapping;

none of it, no:

if you lie on the grass in the dead of summer, and sleep, your body
    heavier than stone, and wake to the sound of something
    tapping and tapping like a sculptor's tool on stone, and look up
    from your dream to see a sparrow hurtling like a missile past
    the stone woman's left breast, right where the arm would have
    been,

    so that it seems for a moment as if the sparrow has destroyed
    the arm or been carried off by it,

    but it is hard to tell, everything is so bright, the woman's body
    blinding against the trees, shining like snow just before dusk, or
    soiled magnolias, or buttermilk, or aged opals, or darkened ice,
    or the full moon, or arms submerged almost to the shoulders
    in a tub of water dark as tea or in the steeping pond;

if you wake on the grass to see a sparrow part the waters of the
    flesh you had forgotten, the milky flesh that pours back for a
    moment after the bird passes—

then the absent arms are heavy;

the arms are so heavy;

not with the dropping down of living arms, falling loosely to the
    side, a rest that contains within it the upward motion that will
    follow, the fingers moving together to grasp and climb an
    unseen rope in the deliberate haphazard way a vine might,

blossoming here and there, fingers and flowers making brief
bright points,

but with the heaviness of something at anchor:

the giant carp, say, grim gold, far gone, who has circled the pond's
floor for years, lying at last taken on the grass, a creature so
pompous and ornate it looks more like a painted figurehead
than a fish, and so huge it seems to drag the foul pond it will
soon be returned to behind it like some ancient and beautiful
ship;

or heavy as a tapestry carried up from some dark crypt into the light
that will reveal—when the bristling cloth that smells of fox fur
and lilies is unrolled— the still golden image of a swooning
dove, its breast impaled by a silver cross;

or heavy as the bodies of twin deer, frozen in midflight, creatures
small and narrow as overbred dogs, and white as lamb's wool,
the dreamy fetish of some man rich beyond measure or
purpose raised to such elegant tomfoolery it fills us with
delight, the way the museum's one prize possession, a life-sized
mechanical silver swan, fills us with delight each time the key is
turned and the bird arches his stiff and handsome neck over
and claps from the mirror that makes his pretty bed a silver
fish, and swallows it, as if he were swallowing a sword, or fire—
making us laugh each time without fail, as if we, too, were fed
on silver fish, or the gardener's sprinklers had just shot on, or
some fool rabbit were rocketing away from an imaginery
hound for the sheer deranged pleasure of it;

heavy as twin deer, the arms held out as an offering for the stone
woman, who may, for all we know, be a goddess, for all we
know, so old she is, so high above;

or heavy as coffers carved in the shape of deer, full of pearls and
    coins, and inlaid with cobalt and ivory patterns, like the
    patterns inside the dome of the mosque, mosaics in dark blue,
    and lighter blue, and white, or the dome of heaven, dead heavy
    with the jewels of heaven, or the Sea of Marmara, the moving
    patterns of the waves, the vast mosaic of scent and sound, fish
    oil and salt, blood and honey tangled with voices calling people
    to prayer and the brutal gulls' cries and the endless sighs of
    shadows slipping across the grass;

heavy the arms, and heavy the arms' white gleam—

the gleam of snowberries, or eyes veiled over and gifted with second
    sight, or smoke from burning roses, or the scrolls of the altar
    wrapped in snowy wool, or the fairest flesh of the fairest child,
    born to be king, and carried into the dark trees by one brave
    and foolish woman who will later be punished as thieves are
    punished, but always her smile will hover in the air, as it
    hovered over the child, the way we hover over the past, bring it
    to life, or find, to our surprise, that it has a life of its own,
    turning and turning in space;

all the imaginings, sweet god, the many arms of the mind, the
    many-mindedness of the spirit descending upon itself, making
    a fullness that seeks entrance and when entrance is found
    unable—like water driven up from below—to resist the
    opening, and so it shoots out, a blossoming of sparrows gone
    mad, making a blessing, the soft spatter of the fountain's water
    upon water in the dead of the afternoon, and one sleeps, and
    then wakes, damp, as if bathed in the sweat of the lover, after
    dreaming of this or that, a darkness through which something
    white floats, a drowned boy, or lilies, or the languid notes of an
    ivory harp, or clouds of perfumed incense, or twin fawns
    breaking from cover, or the mime dance of arms cut loose
    from the body;

one wakes bathed in scented oil to see a sparrow part the waters, or
   move a mountain, or open a gate, yes, open twin gates, narrow
   walls of stone that lead into this city or that, gates called *Eyes of
   the World*, or *Blood Fully Borne*, or *Morning Waking Unto Morning*,
   or *Garden of Unearthly Delights*,

and the mind clears—mayflies, the last fruits of the season,
   trembling in the air above, like the air itself made visible—

and something comes through the gates....what?....what is it?....Oh,
   yes, it is a woman,

no, it is two women,

and they are laughing and laughing, and carrying on.

Acknowledgments

Grateful acknowledgment is made to the editors of the following journals and anthologies, in which these poems appeared:

Another Chicago Magazine: "Lion";
The Antioch Review: "The Dance";
The Carolina Quarterly: "Black Swan";
Journal of New Jersey Poets: "Blessed Is the Field";
The Kenyon Review: "Rose of Sharon," "The Satyr's Heart," "Two Boys," "Windfall";
The Massachusetts Review: "Brightness from the North";
Michigan Quarterly Review: "The Garden of the Trumpet Tree";
New England Review: "The Dragon," "The Foreskin," "The Orchard," "The Sparrow's Gate";
The Recorder: The Journal of the American Irish Historical Society: "Masque," "Midwinter," "Pale Rider," "Plants Fed On by Fawns," "The Rain's Consort," "The South Gate";
Salt Hill: "Sheet Music";
Tamaqua: "Blacklegs";
Third Coast: "Sheep Child";
32 Poems: "The Wolf";
TriQuarterly: "Elegy."

"The Orchard" appeared in *The Best American Poetry 1997*, edited by David Lehman and John Hollander. "The Dragon" appeared in *The Best American Poetry 2003*, edited by David Lehman and Yusef Komunyakaa. "Blacklegs," "Elegy," The Satyr's Heart," "Sheet Music," and "The South Gate," appeared in *Hammer and Blaze*, edited by Ellen Bryant Voigt and Heather McHugh. "Elegy" received a Literary Award from the Illinois Arts Council. "The Orchard" and "Black Swan" appeared in *The New Bread Loaf Anthology of Contemporary Poetry,* edited by Stanley Plumly and Michael Collier. "Black Swan," "Elegy," and "Two Boys" appeared in *Poets of the New Century*, edited by Rick

Higgerson and Roger Weingarten. "Blacklegs" appeared in *The Pushcart Prize XXII: Best of the Small Presses*. "The Dragon" appeared in *The Pushcart Prize XXVIII: Best of the Small Presses*.

I am grateful to The Whiting Foundation, The National Endowment for the Arts, and the Illinois Arts Council for fellowships that supported the writing of this volume; and to the Center for Advanced Study, the English Department, and the Research Board at the University of Illinois for their generous support. Many many thanks also to my patient friends and family—Huck, Maria, Mack, Billy, Marcia, Max, Norma, Deborah, Joy, Marianne, Michael, John, Paul, C. Dale, and Father Ray—to my editors at BOA—Thom Ward and Steve Huff—and to my wonderful students. A special thanks to the Stonington Village Improvement Association and the late James Merrill for the invaluable experience afforded me by a residency at the James Merrill house in Stonington, Connecticut.

About the Author

Brigit Pegeen Kelly teaches in the creative writing program at the University of Illinois in Urbana-Champaign. Her first volume of poetry, *To the Place of Trumpets*, was awarded the Yale Series of Younger Poets Prize in 1987 and published by Yale University Press the following year. Her second book, *Song*, published by BOA Editions, Ltd., was the 1994 Lamont Poetry Selection from the Academy of American Poets and was a finalist for the *Los Angeles Times* Book Award. Her work has appeared widely in journals and anthologies and she has been awarded many prizes and fellowships, including a Whiting Award, two fellowships from the National Endowment for the Arts, The Witter Bynner Prize from the Academy of Arts and Letters, and grants from the Illinois Arts Council and the New Jersey State Council on the Arts.

BOA EDITIONS, LTD.

AMERICAN POETS CONTINUUM SERIES

No. 1   *The Fuhrer Bunker: A Cycle
         of Poems in Progress*
         W. D. Snodgrass

No. 2   *She*
         M. L. Rosenthal

No. 3   *Living With Distance*
         Ralph J. Mills, Jr.

No. 4   *Not Just Any Death*
         Michael Waters

No. 5   *That Was Then: New and
         Selected Poems*
         Isabella Gardner

No. 6   *Things That Happen Where
         There Aren't Any People*
         William Stafford

No. 7   *The Bridge of Change:
         Poems 1974–1980*
         John Logan

No. 8   *Signatures*
         Joseph Stroud

No. 9   *People Live Here: Selected
         Poems 1949–1983*
         Louis Simpson

No. 10   *Yin*
         Carolyn Kizer

No. 11   *Duhamel: Ideas of Order in
         Little Canada*
         Bill Tremblay

No. 12   *Seeing It Was So*
         Anthony Piccione

No. 13   *Hyam Plutzik: The Collected
         Poems*

No. 14   *Good Woman: Poems and a
         Memoir 1969–1980*
         Lucille Clifton

No. 15   *Next: New Poems*
         Lucille Clifton

No. 16   *Roxa: Voices of the Culver
         Family*
         William B. Patrick

No. 17   *John Logan: The Collected Poems*

No. 18   *Isabella Gardner: The
         Collected Poems*

No. 19   *The Sunken Lightship*
         Peter Makuck

No. 20   *The City in Which I Love You*
         Li-Young Lee

No. 21   *Quilting: Poems 1987–1990*
         Lucille Clifton

No. 22   *John Logan: The Collected Fiction*

No. 23   *Shenandoah and Other Verse Plays*
         Delmore Schwartz

No. 24   *Nobody Lives on Arthur
         Godfrey Boulevard*
         Gerald Costanzo

No. 25   *The Book of Names:
         New and Selected Poems*
         Barton Sutter

No. 26   *Each in His Season*
         W. D. Snodgrass

No. 27   *Wordworks: Poems Selected and New*
         Richard Kostelanetz

No. 28   *What We Carry*
         Dorianne Laux

No. 29   *Red Suitcase*
         Naomi Shihab Nye

No. 30   *Song*
         Brigit Pegeen Kelly

No. 31   *The Fuehrer Bunker:
         The Complete Cycle*
         W. D. Snodgrass

No. 32   *For the Kingdom*
         Anthony Piccione

No. 33   *The Quicken Tree*
         Bill Knott

No. 34   *These Upraised Hands*
         William B. Patrick

No. 35   *Crazy Horse in Stillness*
         William Heyen

No. 36   *Quick, Now, Always*
         Mark Irwin

No. 37 *I Have Tasted the Apple*
Mary Crow

No. 38 *The Terrible Stories*
Lucille Clifton

No. 39 *The Heat of Arrivals*
Ray Gonzalez

No. 40 *Jimmy & Rita*
Kim Addonizio

No. 41 *Green Ash, Red Maple,*
Black Gum
Michael Waters

No. 42 *Against Distance*
Peter Makuck

No. 43 *The Night Path*
Laurie Kutchins

No. 44 *Radiography*
Bruce Bond

No. 45 *At My Ease: Uncollected Poems*
of the Fifties and Sixties
David Ignatow

No. 46 *Trillium*
Richard Foerster

No. 47 *Fuel*
Naomi Shihab Nye

No. 48 *Gratitude*
Sam Hamill

No. 49 *Diana, Charles, & the Queen*
William Heyen

No. 50 *Plus Shipping*
Bob Hicok

No. 51 *Cabato Sentora*
Ray Gonzalez

No. 52 *We Didn't Come Here for This*
William B. Patrick

No. 53 *The Vandals*
Alan Michael Parker

No. 54 *To Get Here*
Wendy Mnookin

No. 55 *Living Is What I Wanted: Last Poems*
David Ignatow

No. 56 *Dusty Angel*
Michael Blumenthal

No. 57 *The Tiger Iris*
Joan Swift

No. 58 *White City*
Mark Irwin

No. 59 *Laugh at the End of the World:*
Collected Comic Poems 1969–1999
Bill Knott

No. 60 *Blessing the Boats: New and*
Selected Poems: 1988–2000
Lucille Clifton

No. 61 *Tell Me*
Kim Addonizio

No. 62 *Smoke*
Dorianne Laux

No. 63 *Parthenopi: New and Selected Poems*
Michael Waters

No. 64 *Rancho Notorious*
Richard Garcia

No. 65 *Jam*
Joe-Anne McLaughlin

No. 66 *A. Poulin, Jr. Selected Poems*
Edited, with an Introduction
by Michael Waters

No. 67 *Small Gods of Grief*
Laure-Anne Bosselaar

No. 68 *Book of My Nights*
Li-Young Lee

No. 69 *Tulip Farms and Leper Colonies*
Charles Harper Webb

No. 70 *Double Going*
Richard Foerster

No. 71 *What He Took*
Wendy Mnookin

No. 72 *The Hawk Temple at Tierra Grande*
Ray Gonzalez

No. 73 *Mules of Love*
Ellen Bass

No. 74 *The Guests at the Gate*
Anthony Piccione

No. 75 *Dumb Luck*
Sam Hamill

No. 76 *Love Song with Motor Vehicles*
Alan Michael Parker

No. 77 *Life Watch*
Willis Barnstone

No. 78   *The Owner of the House: New*
         Collected Poems 1940–2001
         Louis Simpson

No. 79   *Is*
         Wayne Dodd

No. 80   *Late*
         Cecilia Woloch

No. 81   *Precipitates*
         Debra Kang Dean

No. 82   *The Orchard*
         Brigit Pegeen Kelly

Colophon

The Orchard, Poems by Brigit Pegeen Kelly,
was set by Richard Foerster, York Beach, Maine,
using Monotype Dante. The cover
was designed by Daphne Poulin-Stofer.
The cover art is courtesy of The J. Paul Getty Museum.
Manufacturing was by McNaughton & Gunn, Saline, Michigan.

The publication of this book was made possible in part by the
special support of the following individuals:

Jeanne Braham
J. Christine Wilson & Mary K. Collins
Dr. and Mrs. Gary H. Conners
Wyn Cooper • Susan De Witt Davie
Ronald & Susan Dow
Brooks DuBose • Pat Ford
Dr. Henry & Beverly French
Judy & Dane Gordon
Marge & Don Grinols
Kip & Deb Hale
Peter & Robin Hursh
Robert & Willy Hursh
Laurie Kutchins • Archie & Pat Kutz
Rosemary & Lew Lloyd
John & Barbara Lovenheim
Phil Memmer
Boo Poulin
Deborah Ronnen • George Wallace
Pat & Michael Wilder
Mark Williams